EARTH

Francis Spencer

A Crabtree Seedlings Book

Table of Contents

Our Home in the Solar System............. 4
Orbiting and Spinning..............................10
Earth's Layers 16
Glossary...23
Index...23

Our Home in the Solar System

In our solar system there is only one **star**. We call this star the Sun. Earth and seven other planets **orbit** the Sun.

The Sun's **gravity** holds all eight planets in their orbit.

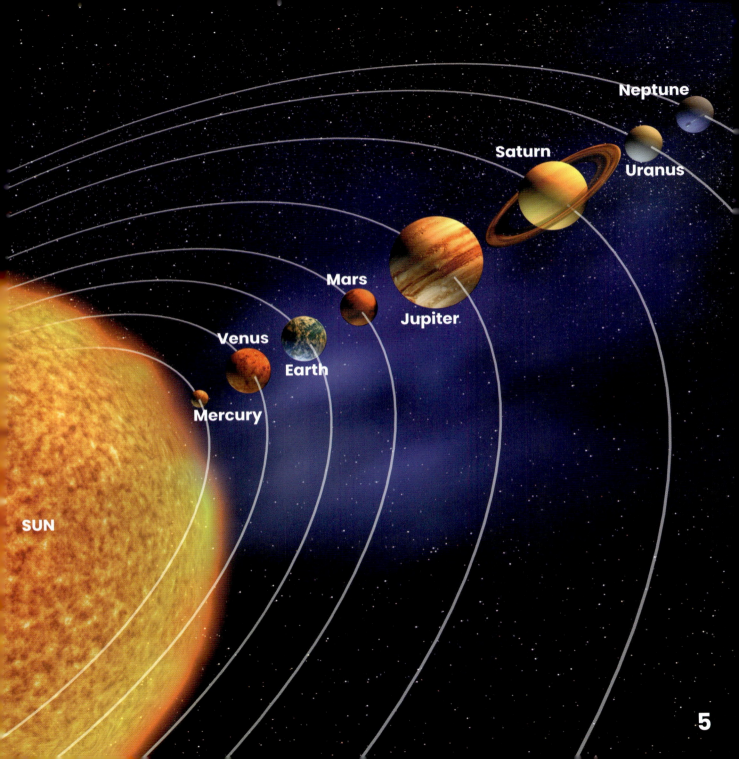

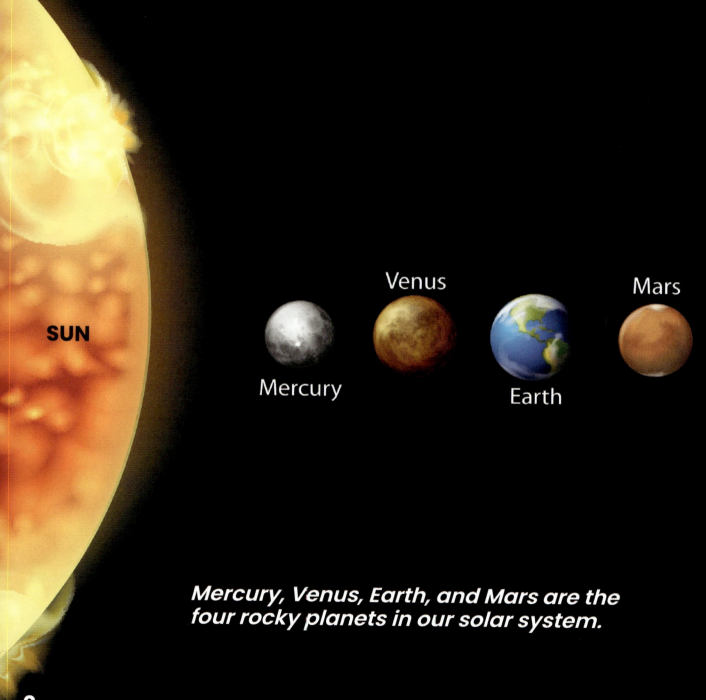

Mercury, Venus, Earth, and Mars are the four rocky planets in our solar system.

Earth is the third planet from the Sun. It is one of the four **rocky planets** in our solar system.

Rocky planets are also called terrestrial planets.

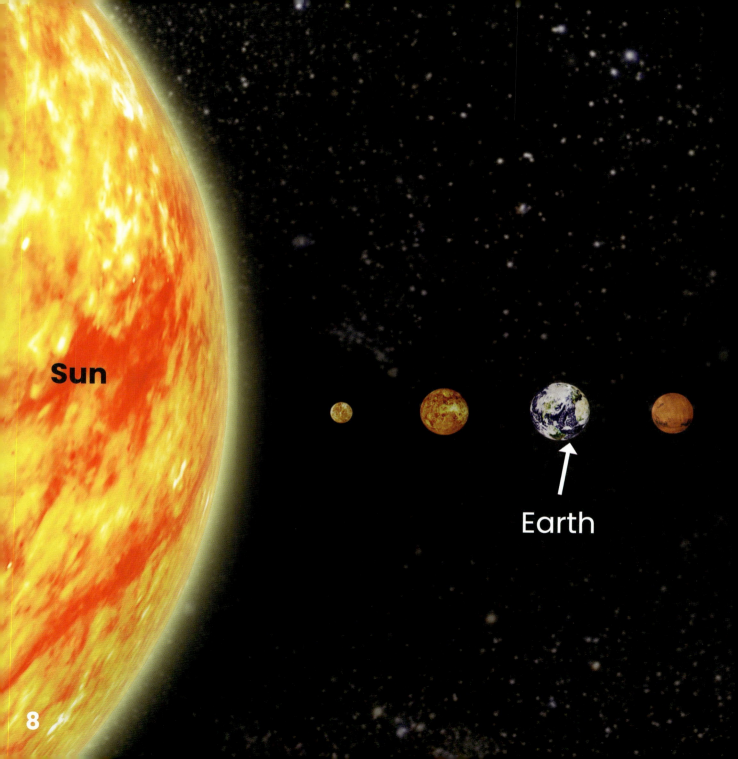

Earth is the perfect distance from the Sun. This means Earth's **temperature** is not too hot, or too cold, for life to exist.

Earth is 93 million miles (150 million kilometers) away from the Sun.

Orbiting and Spinning

It takes Earth a whole year to make a complete orbit around the Sun. As Earth moves around the Sun, it is also spinning on its axis.

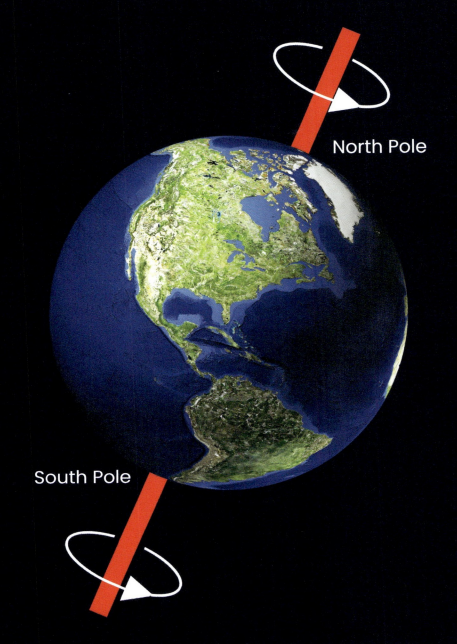

Earth's axis is an invisible line that runs through Earth between the North and South poles.

11

One full turn, or spin, on Earth's axis takes 24 hours. Within that 24 hours we see the sunrise that begins our day and the sunset that begins our night.

Sun

Earth

Because Earth spins, everybody gets a daytime and a nighttime. It is daytime on the side of Earth facing the Sun. It is nighttime on the side of Earth facing away from the Sun.

Earth is **tilted** on its axis. This makes different areas of Earth closer to or farther from the Sun at different times. This is why we have seasons.

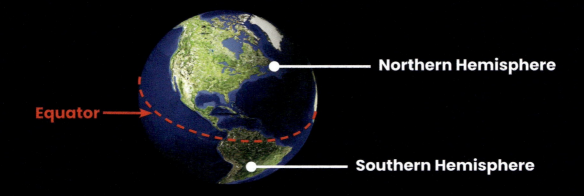

In summer, the Sun shines more directly on the Northern Hemisphere. In winter, the Sun shines more directly on the Southern Hemisphere.

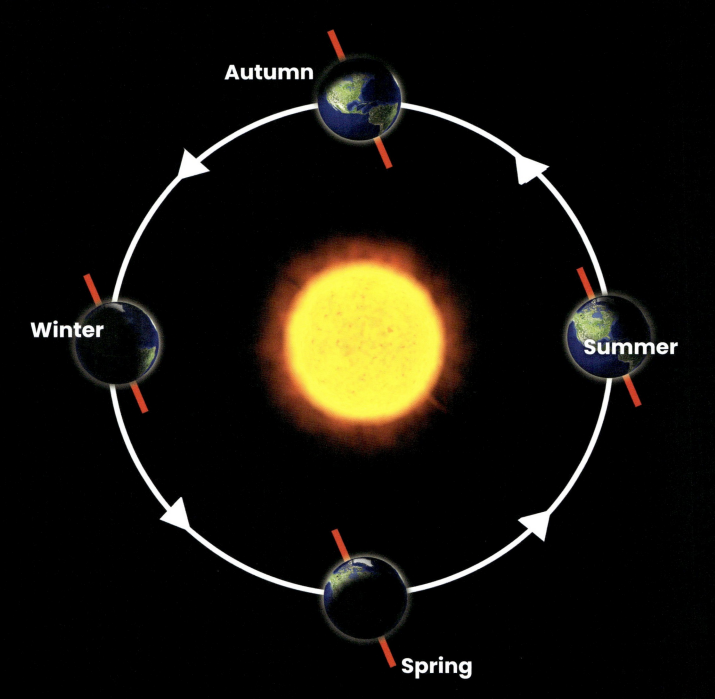

Earth's Layers

Like all the rocky planets, Earth has a rocky outer layer and a metal core. The rocky outer layer is called the crust.

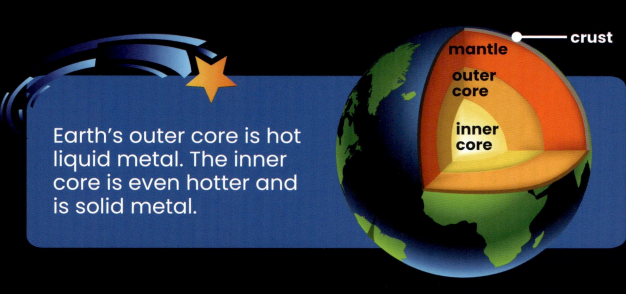

Earth's outer core is hot liquid metal. The inner core is even hotter and is solid metal.

Earth's crust is covered in mountains, deserts, grassy plains, and oceans.

17

Molten rock, called magma, is stored in Earth's crust. When a volcano erupts, magma gets pushed to the surface and spills out as hot lava.

The mantle is between the crust and the outer core. It is mostly solid or semi-solid rock.

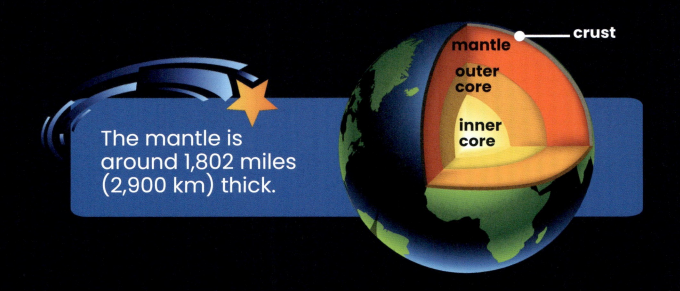

The mantle is around 1,802 miles (2,900 km) thick.

Almost three quarters of Earth's surface is covered in water. Without water, there would be no life on Earth.

From space, the oceans make Earth look like a big blue marble.

Earth is protected by a layer of gases called the **atmosphere**.

Earth's temperature, water, and atmosphere make it the perfect place for us to live.

atmosphere

Glossary

atmosphere (AT-muhss-fihr): A layer of gases around a planet.

gravity (GRAV-uh-tee): The force that holds the planets in our solar system in their orbit.

orbit (OR-bit): To travel in an invisible path around a larger object like a planet or star.

rocky planets (ROK-ee PLAN-its): Planets mostly made of rock and metals.

star (STAR): A ball of burning gases.

temperature (TEM-pur-uh-chur): A measurement of how hot or how cold something is.

tilted (TILT-id): Tipped or slanted to one side.

Index

atmosphere 22
axis 10, 11, 12, 14
core 16, 19
crust 16, 17, 18, 19
day 12, 13
mantle 16, 19
night 12, 13
orbit 4, 10
planet(s) 4, 6, 7, 16
seasons 14

School-to-Home Support for Caregivers and Teachers

This book helps children grow by letting them practice reading. Here are a few guiding questions to help the reader build his or her comprehension skills. Possible answers appear here in red.

Before Reading
- **What do I think this book is about?** I think this book is filled with many facts about the planet Earth. I think this book is about Earth's position in the solar system.
- **What do I want to learn about this topic?** I want to learn about going into outer space. I want to learn more about the different layers of Earth.

During Reading
- **I wonder why...** I wonder why Earth is called a rocky planet. I wonder why Earth tilts on its axis.

- **What have I learned so far?** I have learned that Earth is about 93 million miles away (150 million km) from the Sun. I have learned that Earth is the third planet from the Sun.

After Reading
- **What details did I learn about this topic?** I have learned that it takes Earth a whole year to make a complete orbit around the Sun. I have learned that Earth is protected by a layer of gases called the atmosphere.
- **Read the book again and look for the glossary words.** I see the word *temperature* on page 9, and the word *tilted* on page 14. The other glossary words are found on page 23.

Library and Archives Canada Cataloguing in Publication

CIP available at Library and Archives Canada

Library of Congress Cataloging-in-Publication Data

CIP available at Library of Congress

Crabtree Publishing Company
www.crabtreebooks.com   1–800–387–7650

Written by: Francis Spencer

Production coordinator and Prepress technician: Tammy McGarr

Print coordinator: Katherine Berti

Print book version produced jointly with Blue Door Education in 2022

Printed in the U.S.A./CG20210915/012022

Content produced and published by Blue Door Education, Melbourne Beach FL USA. This title Copyright Blue Door Education. All rights reserved. No part of this book may be reproduced or utilized in any form or by any means, electronic or mechanical including photocopying, recording, or by any information storage and retrieval system without permission in writing from the publisher.

PHOTO CREDITS:
Cover © MarcelClemens ; star graphic on most pages © Gleb Guralnyk; pages 2-3 © ibreakstock, page 5 © Orla; page 6 © BlueRingMedia; page 8-9 © Bobboz; page 11, 14 and 15 © Iboo07; page 13 © sebikus; page 16 and 19 ©Webspark; page 7 © infografick; page 18 © beboy; page 21 © MarcelClemens; page 23 ©Anton Balazh All images from Shutterstock.com

Published in the United States
Crabtree Publishing
347 Fifth Ave.
Suite 1402-145
New York, NY 10016

Published in Canada
Crabtree Publishing
616 Welland Ave.
St. Catharines, Ontario
L2M 5V6